DEALING WITH CRIME

Judith Anderson

First published in 2005 by
Franklin Watts
96 Leonard Street
London
EC2A 4XD

Franklin Watts Australia
Level 17/207 Kent Street
Sydney NSW 2000

ISBN: 0 7496 6309 X
Dewey Classification: 364

Series editor: Sarah Peutrill
Art director: Jonathan Hair
Design: Proof Books
Picture researcher: Sophie Hartley

Picture and text credits: see page 48.

Note on websites:
Every effort has been made by the Publishers to ensure that the websites in this book contain no inappropriate or offensive material. However, because of the nature of the Internet, it is impossible to guarantee that the contents of these sites will not be altered. We strongly advise that Internet access is supervised by a responsible adult.

A CIP catalogue record for this book is available from the British Library.

Printed in China

Contents

What's the issue?

A universal problem

Crime affects us all. Some experience crime first-hand, either as a victim or as an offender or perhaps as a witness or a police officer. We are all subject to the laws that define crime, and we all make choices about whether or not to break those laws. We are also influenced by fear of crime. Each time we lock our front door or avoid a 'risky' part of town we demonstrate the impact of crime on our society.

The criminal justice system

This book looks at how we deal with crime. It contains strong and often contradictory reactions, because crime touches on some of our most basic rights as human beings – the right to life, the right to liberty, the right to protect ourselves and our possessions. The task of the criminal justice system – including the police, the courts, and prison services – is to balance these rights so that the victim sees justice done, the innocent are protected, and the accused are tried fairly and without prejudice. It is a difficult task.

Statistics

The statistics used in this book reveal some of these problems. They are all 'facts' of one sort or another, but they rarely present the whole truth. For example, anti-social behaviour is one of the fastest growing crimes in the UK, but is this because there are new laws against it, or because more people are reporting it, or because more people are committing it?

Yet statistics can reveal important trends and attitudes towards crime. They show, for example, that car theft

is a common crime. They also show that methods of car theft are changing. Because car manufacturers are making new cars more secure, thieves are increasingly breaking into people's homes to steal car keys.

Changing laws

The criminal justice system has to evolve in order to keep pace with changing attitudes and realities. The threat of terrorism, for instance, is now starting to shape new laws and new police powers. Yet change should not come without debate. And at the heart of this debate lies what each of us believes is right and wrong.

Note on quotes

Quotes presented in this book in a specific context should not be understood to commit their source to one side of that debate. They are simply illustrations of the possible viewpoints in each debate.

Further information

Websites for further information are given throughout the book. A good general website is www.rizer.co.uk. This site is designed specifically for young people, providing information and advice about the law, crime and the consequences of offending.

French police survey a beach – beaches are one of the most common places for crimes, especially theft, to occur.

Q: Is crime more of a problem today than 30 years ago?

MANY PEOPLE say that they are worried about rising crime. The evidence seems to be everywhere – in the media, on CCTV, in overcrowded prisons. Yet the statistics on crime are not clear-cut. Variations in the type of crime, whether it is reported and how it is recorded mean that comparisons with the past can be unreliable. However, some new types of crime have spread rapidly in the past 30 years, including 'cybercrime' such as identity fraud, and mobile phone crime.

A young boy holds a sign protesting against violence in Venezuela. Several thousand people marched to protest about the government's failure to tackle a wave of violent crime.

YES

'Studies made in previous years predicted that by 1998, America would see a dramatic increase in crimes committed by juveniles. Well folks, we're beginning to see it! And it's not over yet.'

Vic Bilson, anti-liberal campaigner, USA

'I've been mugged three times in the past two years – twice for my mobile phone. Who says things are getting better? I don't feel nearly as safe as I did ten years ago.'

Irish mugging victim

'Data espionage and data theft, credit card fraud, child pornography, far-right extremism and terrorists are ever more common on the Internet.'

Joschka Fischer, German Foreign Minister

STATISTICALLY SPEAKING

- In 2003, 73% of those questioned in the British Crime Survey said they believed crime was increasing. In fact, overall crime figures were down on the previous year by 3%, but violent crime was up by 2%.

NO

'I haven't seen such continuous drops in so many categories of crime over such a long period.'

Don Weatherburn, Director of the Bureau of Crime Statistics and Research, commenting on the third annual drop in crime in 2004 in New South Wales, Australia

✖ 'The overall picture of crime in Canada looks very much like it did last year and the year before that ... It does not support claims by some people that Canada is becoming a more violent place.'

Criminologist Rosemary Gartner, University of Toronto, Canada

✖ 'The only real crime trend is increasing crime coverage. Between 1990 and 1995 there was a 240% increase in network news coverage of murders, even though the Justice Department reported that there was a 13% decline in homicides in that period.'

Vincent Schiraldi, Director of the Justice Policy Institute, USA

STATISTICALLY SPEAKING

Serious violent crime levels in the USA 1973–2003

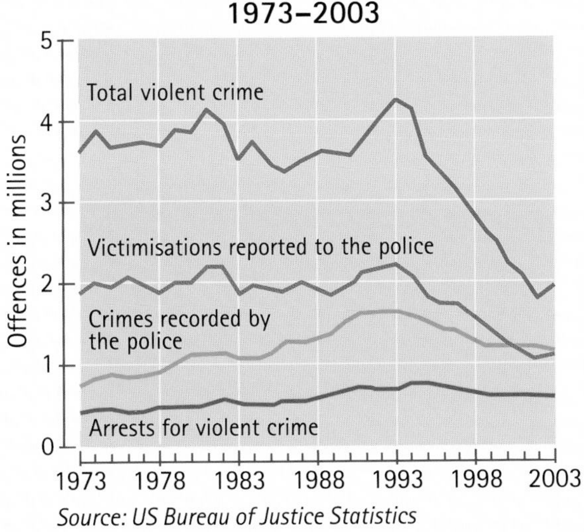

Source: US Bureau of Justice Statistics

CONFLICTING EVIDENCE?

'Britain continues to be one of the safest places in the world to live.'

UK Home Office press release, 2001

Percentage of people who were victims of violent assault, robbery, theft of a car or burglary once or more in one year:

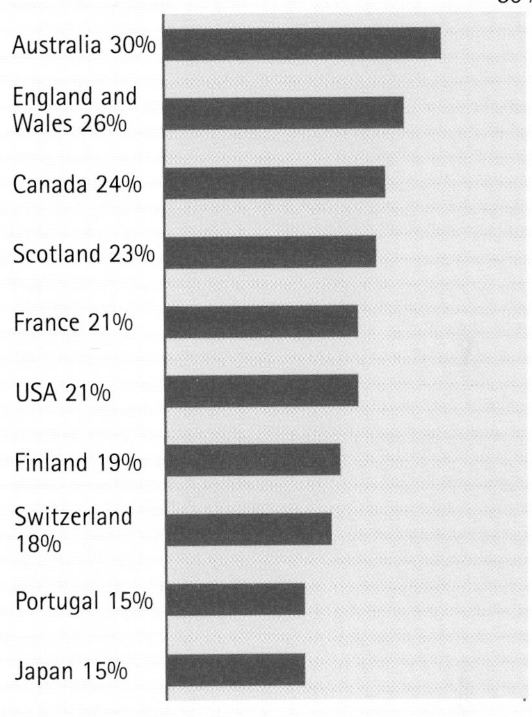

Source: International Crime Victims Survey

MORE TO THINK ABOUT

The British Crime Survey does not include the under-16s. Yet this is the fastest growing group of both offenders and victims of crime in the UK. The peak hour for street crimes is not at night when the bars and pubs close, but between 4 pm and 5 pm when schools close.

FIND OUT MORE: www.homeoffice.gov.uk www.aic.gov.au www.ojp.usdoj.gov/bjs www.bbc.co.uk/crime

Q: Is deprivation an excuse for crime?

LINKS BETWEEN deprivation (extreme poverty) and crime have been accepted for many years. However, such links do not prove that deprivation is a cause of crime, or that it is an excuse. Many would argue that a starving child who steals food should not be treated as a criminal. But what of the teenager who commits arson because he was excluded from school, or the woman who shoplifts because she is unemployed and depressed?

A homeless woman in Russia. Increasing poverty and homelessness have been linked to high crime rates in Russia.

YES 'Gary Graham's life is a testament to the unacceptable price society pays for ... generational poverty, racial prejudice, sub-standard schools, job discrimination ...'

Richard Burr, legal counsel for Gary Graham, a black American executed for murder

✓ 'We worked with one young woman who had become involved in prostitution, and subsequently drug abuse, at the age of 13, because ... her mum introduced her to various men so that the family could afford to eat.'

Daljeet Dagon, Streetwork Team, Scotland

✓ 'You don't have to probe very far into the backgrounds of children who wind up in police stations and courtrooms to find a common denominator: poverty.'

Lisbet Palme, UNICEF

NO

'I am sick of social deprivation being used as an excuse to justify crime. It's insulting. My parents were hard up and living on a council estate when my sister and I grew up, but you don't see us out mugging, stealing and vandalising.'

Dan, BBC Online 'Have Your Say'

'Poverty may provide the environment for some crime, but it should not provide an excuse. Greed and selfishness are also principal causes.'

Pastoral letter from the Catholic bishops of New Zealand

'As great as my compassion for Robert Harris the child, I cannot excuse nor forgive the choice made by Robert Harris the man.'

California Governor Pete Wilson's response to an appeal for Robert Harris, who murdered two teenagers in the USA. Robert Harris suffered physical abuse throughout his childhood

STATISTICALLY SPEAKING

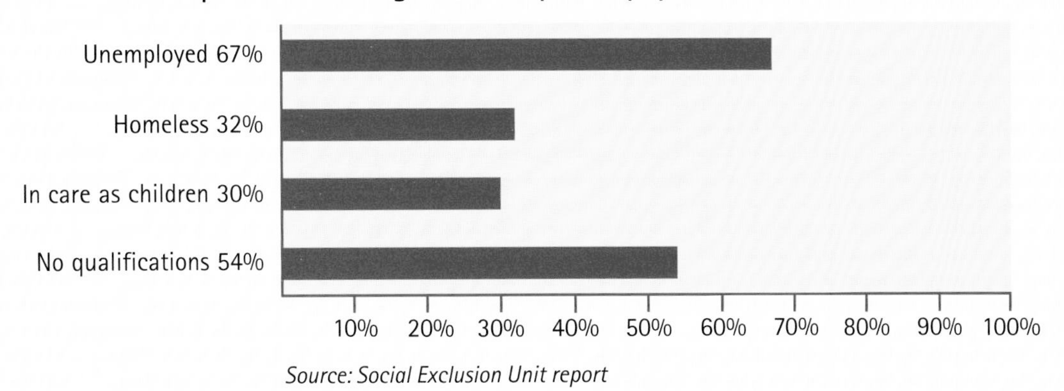

Source: Social Exclusion Unit report

CASE STUDY

RACHEL'S STORY

Rachel was rejected by her mother when she was seven years old. She lived in four different children's homes, and ran away aged 16. She had no money and was 'befriended' by a drug addict. Within a week she was taking drugs herself, and soon began stealing to pay for her habit. Two years later she began a prison sentence for theft and shoplifting offences.

MORE TO THINK ABOUT

While many deprived areas have high crime rates some deprived areas have very low crime rates. These areas are typified by long-established communities in rural or semi-rural areas. The highest crime rates occur in areas of inner-city deprivation. What reasons might there be for this?

Q: Do we need more police on the streets?

MANY PEOPLE believe that more police, with a more visible presence in the local community, leads to less crime. They point to community policing initiatives in the USA, where a 'zero-tolerance' approach to minor offences such as vandalism may have contributed to a recent drop in overall crime. However, some argue that too many police can increase conflict within communities. Others point out that putting more police on the streets may mean fewer police working on 'hidden' crimes such as fraud or child abuse.

STATISTICALLY SPEAKING

- A poll conducted in the UK found that 70% of those asked said that more police on the streets would make them feel safer in their area.

YES

'American research has shown that one of the most effective uses of police resources is high visibility at crime hotspots ... In Australia the number of police has failed to keep pace with the escalating crime rate for the past 40 years.'

Nicole Billante, The Centre for Independent Studies, Australia

'We have had a lot of trouble with children down by the shops being abusive. Every now and then the police come round to check everything is OK but they should do it more often.'

Maureen Brookes, resident of a quiet suburb

'The key to creating a safer community is a greater police presence.'

Sarah Teather, Liberal Democrat Member of Parliament, UK

'Put more police on the streets and they'll catch more criminals. It's not rocket science, is it?'

Conservative Party campaign poster, UK

A large police presence at a biotechnology protest in San Francisco, USA. Are large numbers of police at protests necessary?

CONFLICTING EVIDENCE?

Washington DC had 631 police officers per 100,000 population in 2000 – the highest ratio of police in the US. It also had one of the highest murder rates in the US and, between 1990 and 2000, the percentage of crimes solved in Washington DC dropped from 57% to 36%.

Source: The Washington Post

Percentage change in number of crimes and number of full-time police officers in large cities in the USA between 1990 and 2000:

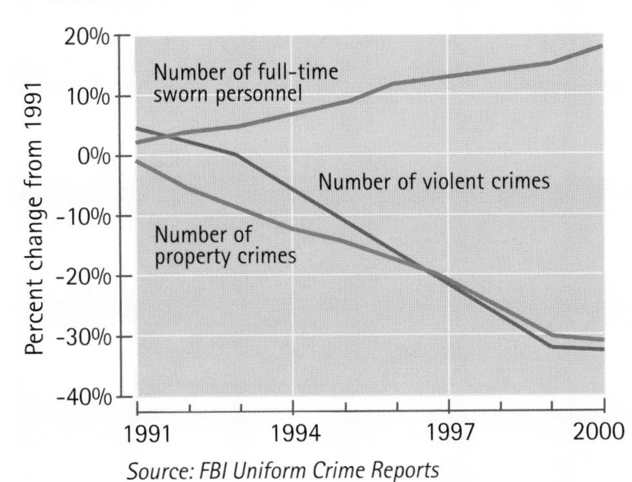

Source: FBI Uniform Crime Reports

NO

'It is very difficult to see a direct connection between increasing numbers of police officers and automatically solving one particular area of crime.'

Zaki Hashmi, British criminal lawyer

✖ 'Zero tolerance is nothing more than old fashioned law and order along with the traditional over-policing of poor and marginal social groups.'

Tim Anderson, New South Wales Council for Civil Liberties, Australia

✖ 'Giuliani = Police State'

Message chalked on the street by Robert Lederman in protest at Mayor Giuliani's police 'crackdown' on crime in New York, USA

MORE TO THINK ABOUT

It might be argued that police numbers themselves have little effect on crime; what matters is effective policing. What do you think is the most important aspect of a police officer's job?

FIND OUT MORE: www.polfed.org www.homeoffice.gov.uk/crime www.popcenter.org www.liberty-human-rights.org.uk

Q: Are prison sentences a crime deterrent?

THE EFFECTIVENESS of prison as a deterrent is controversial. Some argue that the more likely a criminal is to be imprisoned, the greater the deterrent. Others argue that it is the length of sentence that counts. However, many ex-prisoners go on to re-offend, and some say that the experience of prison encourages crime. The type of crime also matters. Drug addicts and those who commit violent crimes may be less likely to weigh up the risk of prison before offending.

A prison in Colorado, USA for repeat and high-profile offenders.

NO

'Over 60% of the people inside are just kids, and we are just making them anti-society, anti-good.'

Stephen P Bohrer, former inmate of the California prison system, USA

'Many of these offenders have chronic problems related to drug use ... There are very few formal mechanisms available for such offenders to be linked to community-based services upon release ... Therefore the drug and crime cycle is regularly perpetuated.'

South Australia Department of Correctional Services

'Potential offenders don't seriously take into account getting caught, so it doesn't matter what you're threatening to punish at the other end.'

Professor Paul Robinson, University of Pennsylvania, USA

STATISTICALLY SPEAKING

- In the UK, more than 50% of all prisoners discharged are reconvicted within two years of their release. For young male offenders, the reconviction rate is about 75%. In South Australia, 80% of all prisoners discharged in 2001 had a prior history of imprisonment.

YES 'Spain imprisons four times more people than Scotland relative to recorded crime, and Ireland three times more. Unsurprisingly, the deterrent is such that crimes per capita in both Ireland and Spain is around a quarter of the level in Scotland.'

Annabel Goldie, Member of the Scottish Parliament

'The prospect of prison, more than any other sanction, is feared by white-collar criminals and has a powerful deterrent effect.'

US Deputy Attorney General Larry Thompson

'A Home Office report in 2000 found the average offender carried out 140 offences per year ... If we were to jail 5,000 criminals who would otherwise have committed 140 offences, then 700,000 offences against the public would be prevented by 12 months in jail.'

David Green, Director of the UK Institute for the Study of Civil Society

STATISTICALLY SPEAKING

Burglary rates and incarceration rates in the USA and England/Wales

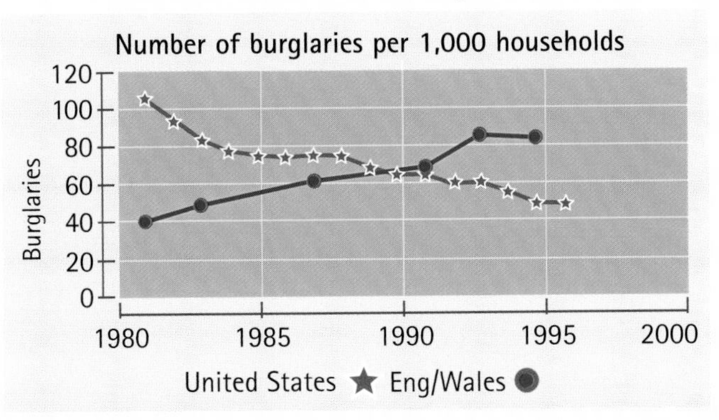

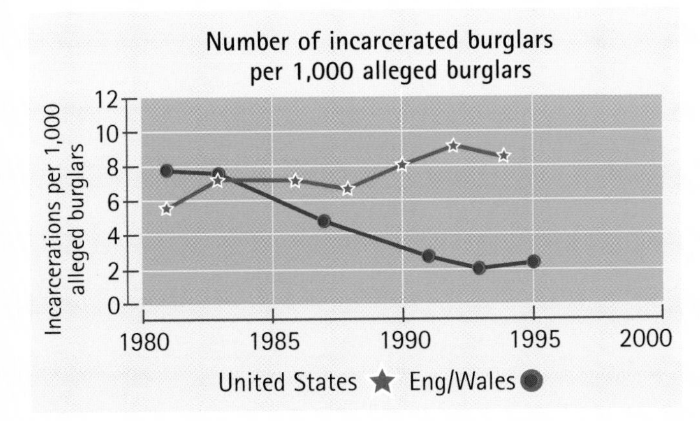

Source: International Crime Victim Survey

CASE STUDY

A YOUNG OFFENDER'S STORY

Levi is an 18-year-old young offender. He has been involved in crime since his early teens.

'I am 18, with two children, who I love and adore very much, but yet again I am in [prison] for a robbery, which was stupid to do. I have been in nearly seven months ... Let me just say one thing, "crime is not worth the hassle of being separated from your loved ones". You might have heard this before but I have learned my lesson. I can guarantee [prison] will not see me again.'

MORE TO THINK ABOUT

In some prisons, as many as four out of five inmates have some kind of psychological disorder. Does mental illness reduce the effectiveness of prison as a deterrent to crime?

FIND OUT MORE: www.prisonreformtrust.org.uk www.pmnw.co.uk www.bop.gov www.sentencingproject.org

Q: Should ID cards be introduced to tackle crime?

IDENTITY (ID) cards are supposed to prove we are who we say we are. Such cards show details such as the holder's name, address, age, benefit entitlements and, in some countries, religion or ethnicity. They often include a photograph, and may now hold 'biometric' data such as iris scans or fingerprints to discourage forgery. Many argue that ID cards can help tackle crime, terrorism and illegal immigration. However, issues of cost, confidentiality and abuse have deterred countries such as the USA and Australia from introducing them.

A Turkish police officer returns an identity card to a Turkish woman at a check-point set up after a series of terrorist attacks in Istanbul in 2000. Suicide bombers killed over 50 people and injured many more.

YES

'A national ID card scheme will provide a "gold standard" for ... protecting individuals from the modern-day crime of identity theft, protecting public services for use by those who are properly entitled to them, and helping us tackle crime, terrorism, and illegal immigration and working.'

David Blunkett, former British Home Secretary

'ID cards are vital in the fight against crime as they enable officers to identify suspects quickly and thereby inconvenience individuals less.'

Mrs Jan Berry, Chair of the Police Federation of England and Wales

'Australia really needs to get serious about a national ID card based on biometric data ... reliance on non-biometric based documents such as passports and drivers' licenses is an invitation to conduct ID fraud.'

Clive Williams, director of terrorism studies, Australian National University

STATISTICALLY SPEAKING

- A poll taken shortly after the September 11th terrorist attacks showed that 68% of Americans favoured a national identity card 'to bolster anti-terrorism concerns'.

CONFLICTING EVIDENCE?

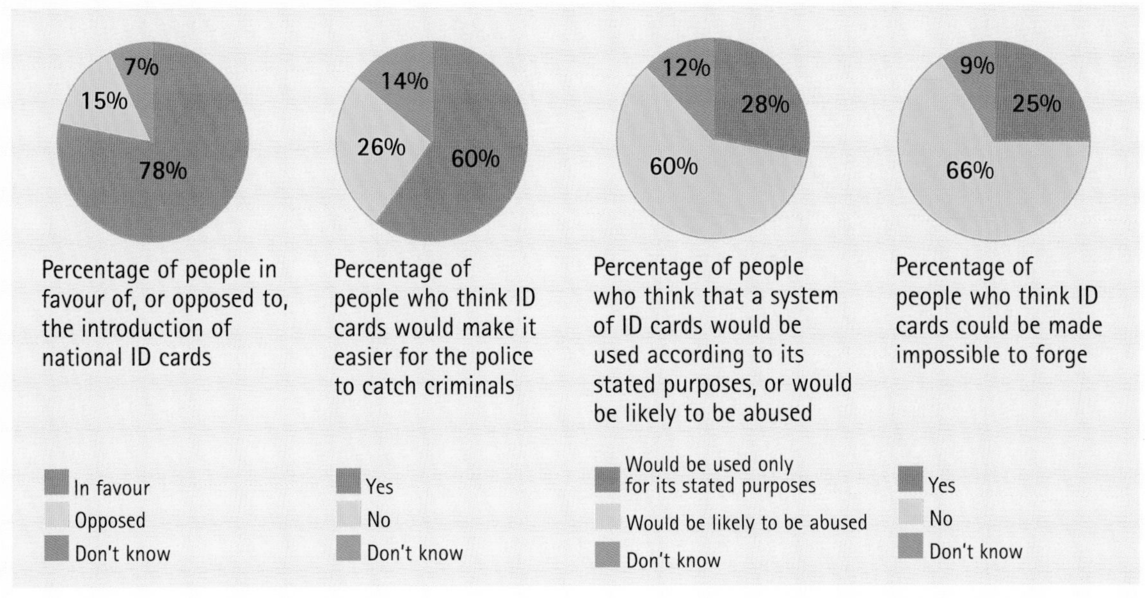

Source: UK YouGov Survey

NO 'A national ID card will not prevent terrorism. It would not have thwarted the September 11 hijackers, for example, many of whom reportedly had identification documents on them, and were in the country legally.'

American Civil Liberties Union

✖ 'No form of documentation is totally secure and "unforgeable". If one (legitimate) person has the technology to make an ID card, then another (illegitimate) person can have it too.'

Adrian Beck, Lecturer in Security Management, University of Leicester, UK

✖ 'The success of ID cards as a means of fighting crime or illegal immigration will depend on a discriminatory checking procedure which will target minorities.'

Simon Davies, Director General of Privacy International

MORE TO THINK ABOUT

This debate raises many issues that have not been covered here. They include: confidentiality, cost, whether children should have ID cards as well as adults, and whether they should be compulsory or voluntary.

Mark Oaten, a British politician, says 'It would be better spending money on the police than a piece of plastic.' What do you think?

FIND OUT MORE: www.privacy.org www.liberty-human-rights.org.uk www.identitycards.gov.uk www.polfed.org

Q: Is the death penalty the best way to fight serious crime?

MANY COUNTRIES around the world have abolished the death penalty (capital punishment), but two of the biggest, the USA and China, still use it. Most supporters of the death penalty do not believe it should be used for all murders, only for the worst crimes such as child murder or premeditated murder. However, those who oppose its use say that it is immoral, ineffective as a deterrent and can lead to the execution of innocent people.

Katerina Koneva was murdered by Andrezej Kunowski, 'the beast of Poland'. He had been released from prison after similar offences. Exercising the death penalty earlier would have prevented her death.

YES

'Any crime which the law regards as serious should certainly receive serious penalties, and any crime which is punishable by the death penalty according to the law, should certainly receive the death penalty.'

Hu Jintao, President of the People's Republic of China

'We have no hate or bitterness in our hearts. But that doesn't mean he does not pay for his crime.'

Vikki Haack, after witnessing the execution of her sister's killer

'If we execute murderers and there is in fact no deterrent effect, we have killed a bunch of murderers. If we fail to execute murderers, and doing so would in fact have deterred other murders, we have allowed the killing of a bunch of innocent victims. I would much rather risk the former.'

John McAdams, Marquette University, USA

STATISTICALLY SPEAKING

- Of the 875 prisoners executed in the USA in modern times, not one has been retroactively proved innocent.

NO

'Amnesty International opposes capital punishment ... Its effectiveness as a unique deterrent to crime has never been proven, and with levels of crime continuing to rise in China, its irrelevance to crime control and prevention cannot be ignored.'

Amnesty International

✖ 'Capital punishment in my view achieved nothing except revenge.'

Albert Pierrepoint, Britain's hangman for 25 years

✖ 'Errors can and have been made repeatedly in the trial of death penalty cases.'

US Congress Subcommittee on Civil and Constitutional Rights

CONFLICTING EVIDENCE?

'Each execution results, on average, in 18 fewer murders – with a margin of error of plus or minus 10.'

Emory University, USA

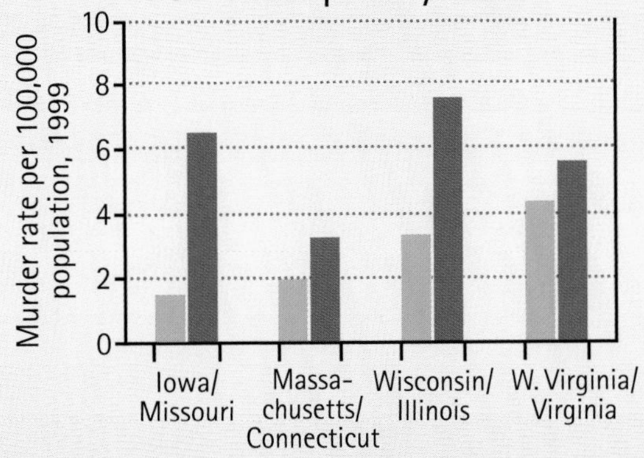

STATISTICALLY SPEAKING

- Between 1973 and 2004, 117 people from 25 US states have been released from death row because of evidence of wrongful conviction.
- A comprehensive study in the USA found that the death penalty costs North Carolina $2.16 million more per execution than a non-death penalty murder case with a sentence of life imprisonment.

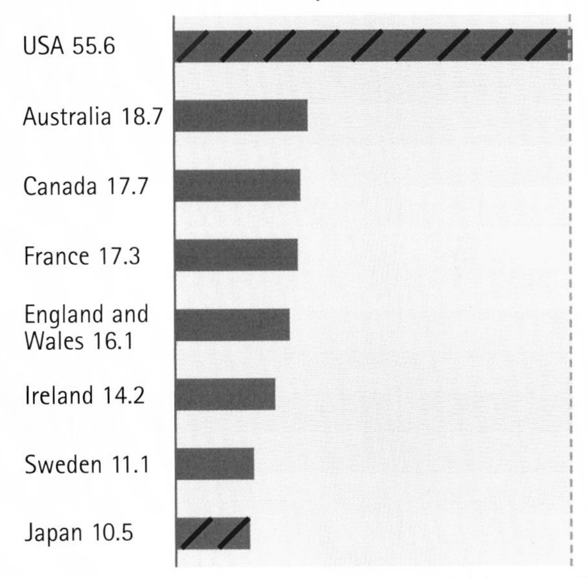

MORE TO THINK ABOUT

There are lots of key issues about the death penalty. This page covers cost, retribution, innocence, victims, morality and deterrence but there are other issues that can be considered, for example: mental illness, race and religious viewpoints.

FIND OUT MORE: www.amnesty.org www.deathpenaltyinfo.org www.prodeathpenalty.com www.dpinfo.com www.mvfr.org

Q: Should prisons be for treatment rather than punishment?

WHAT ARE prisons for? Most countries agree that punishment, deterrence and rehabilitation all play a part. The hope is that when prisoners are released they have not only paid for their crimes but they are somehow 'reformed' and will not re-offend. Studies show that training and treatment can reduce re-offending rates but some argue that the only way to protect society from violent criminals is to lock them up indefinitely.

YES 'We know from long experience that if [former prisoners] can't find work, or a home, or help, they are much more likely to commit more crimes and return to prison ... America is the land of the second chance, and when the gates of the prison open, the path ahead should lead to a better life.'

George W Bush, US President

'It's self-evident in terms of value for money that if we can get people off drugs, on to [reform] programmes and into education, then we're going to reduce crime.'

Martin Narey, director-general of UK Prison Service

'The treatment of persons sentenced to imprisonment shall have as its purpose to establish in them the will to lead law-abiding and self-supporting lives after their release and to fit them to do so.'

UN High Commission for Human Rights

CASE STUDY

THE 'MOORS MURDERESS'

Myra Hindley was sentenced to 25 years in prison for her role in the murders of five children in England in 1956. Her crimes were horrific, but the judge at her trial recommended a limit on her sentence because he believed she had the potential for reform.

During her years in prison she studied for a degree, turned to Christianity and reputedly showed remorse for her crimes. The parole board decided that she no longer represented a threat to society and recommended her release. Nevertheless, public opinion was strongly opposed to Hindley's freedom and successive Home Office ministers used their powers to extend her sentence for an indefinite period. She died in prison in 2002.

NO

'Prison should be a form of punishment not a holiday camp, or a place where murderers can get a degree in psychology at the taxpayers' expense.'

P Olohan, BBC Online 'Talking Point'

✖ 'There are crimes so heinous that we must draw a line in the sand. We must say to criminals, if you commit one of these crimes, you are finished. You don't get a second chance.'

Matt Salmon, Arizona State Representative, speaking in favour of the 'No Second Chances for Murderers, Rapists or Child Molesters' bill

✖ 'What do we do with [sex offenders]? We keep them away from children at whatever cost. If it means incarcerating them for ever, so be it. Don't allow them to be back out amongst children again.'

Wendy Utting, Australian child protection advocate

STATISTICALLY SPEAKING

- In 1996, 6% of US prison budgets were spent on rehabilitation programmes and 94% were for building, staffing and maintaining prisons.

STATISTICALLY SPEAKING

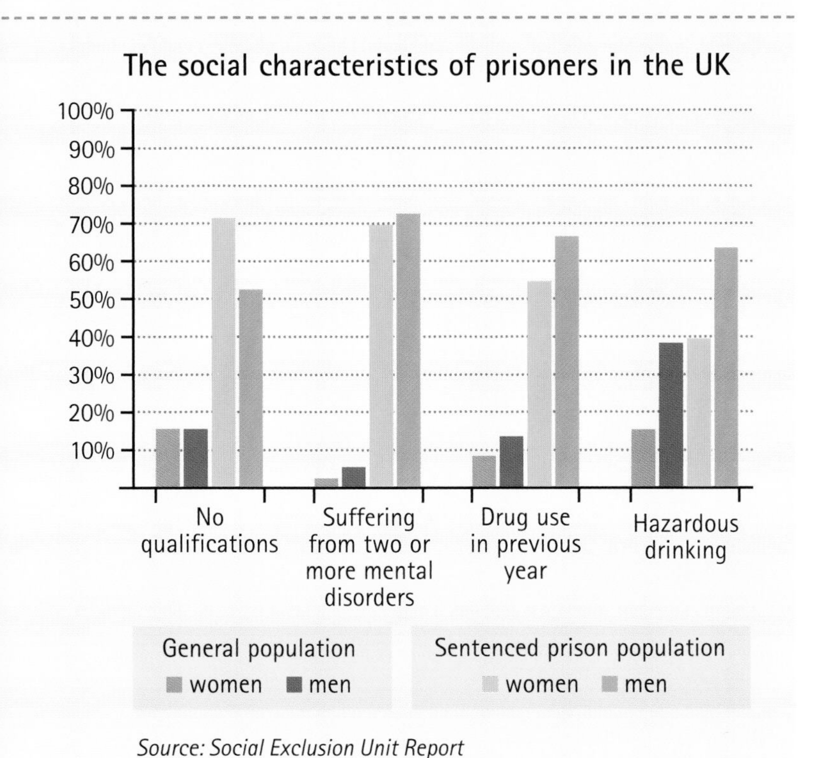

Source: Social Exclusion Unit Report

MORE TO THINK ABOUT

Other points to consider are:

Should drug addicts and the mentally ill be in prison in the first place?

What is the cost to society of treatment and education programmes?

Should release from prison be conditional on participation in a rehabilitation programme?

Q: Is trial by jury the fairest way to reach a verdict?

MANY PEOPLE believe that juries underpin the basic right to a fair trial. While their use differs from country to country, the central principle is that the defendant is judged by a group of his or her peers, so that the verdict is both fair and free from government interference. Nevertheless, some issues can cast doubt on the fairness of jury trials, including corruption, intimidation, prejudice and whether jurors are able to understand the complex evidence in trials involving fraud or technology.

YES

'In all criminal prosecutions, the accused shall enjoy the right to a speedy and public trial, by an impartial jury of the State and district wherein the crime shall have been committed.'

US Constitution: Sixth Amendment

✔ 'Give me a jury any day rather than a case-hardened judge on nodding terms with the police.'

Helena Kennedy, British civil liberties lawyer

✔ 'The research shows that while certain elements of complex trials do tax jurors' comprehension and understanding, there is no firm evidence that their judgements have therefore been wrong. Jurors are capable of solving highly complex cases.'

Robert D Myers, US Judge

NO

'Our proposals for trial by judge alone address the problems in trying a very small number of fraud and complex financial cases. Such trials can last for months on end. They make it difficult to find a representative jury ... Evidence must be pared down, and charges against the defendant reduced, in order to make trials manageable. This cannot be right.'

Lord Falconer, British Minister of State for criminal justice, sentencing and law reform

✖ 'In practice ... juries are massively swayed by one or two vocal individuals. There is also a strong pressure to conform to a unanimous verdict.'

Professor Richard Dawkins, Oxford University, UK

✖ 'In a high profile case like this, and the media grabs hold of it, the evidence has to be so overwhelming before an individual is charged with a case, that I personally kind of lean towards his guilt before we even get started.'

A potential juror's comments during a selection interview at the trial of Theodore Kaczynski, who was found guilty of carrying out a series of deadly bombings in the USA

CONFLICTING EVIDENCE?

'All persons selected for jury service shall be selected at random.'

Superior Court of California, USA

In California in 1995, black celebrity footballer OJ Simpson went on trial for murder.

The selection of jurors was tainted by accusations of racial bias from both sides.

Composition of the initial jury pool

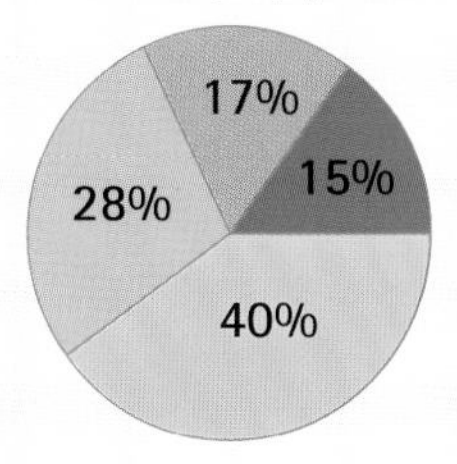

Composition of the final jury selected

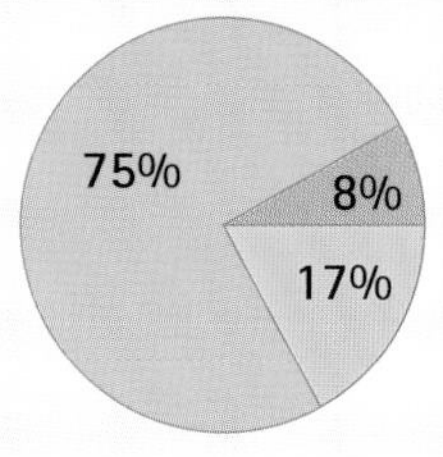

Composition of California's population in 1995:

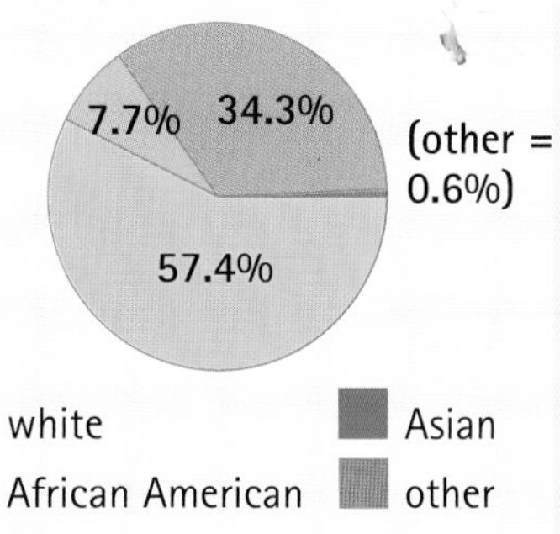

OJ Simpson (centre) was acquitted of murder in a widely-criticised trial.

STATISTICALLY SPEAKING

- In a New Zealand study, trial judges said they would have reached a different verdict to the jury in 24 out of 48 cases. In most cases, the disagreement was over the credibility of key witnesses. In 6 of the 48 cases, jurors said that 'feeling time was running out' or that 'people wanted to get home' were factors in reaching a verdict.

MORE TO THINK ABOUT

In some countries, and in some kinds of trial, a verdict does not have to be unanimous. A majority verdict often prevents a trial from collapsing without a verdict, and it can help to prevent undue pressure being placed on jurors who disagree. However, a majority verdict means that there is some doubt in one or more jurors' minds. Which is fairer?

FIND OUT MORE: www.crfc.org/americanjury www.courts.sa.gov.au www.juror.cjsonline.org www.justice.qld.gov.au/courts/jurors.htm

Q: Is it every adult's right to own a gun?

OWNING A gun means different things to different people. Hunters and farmers say that guns are essential to their livelihoods. Others use guns for sport. Many people think that they should be allowed to own a gun to defend themselves and their property. They argue that this works as a deterrent to crime. However, anti-gun campaigners believe that gun ownership increases gun-related crimes, and that anti-gun laws are essential to protect people from such violence.

Women who behave passively when attacked are 2.5 times more likely to be seriously injured than a woman who has a gun when confronted by a criminal according to Professor John Lott, author of *More Guns Less Crime.*

YES

'A person must have the right to defend his or her life from violence. The right to self-defence is meaningless unless you are able to defend yourself in an effective manner. Thus the right to have arms is ... an expression of the right to life.'

Karen MacNutt, contributing editor, Women & Guns

'A well-regulated Militia being necessary to the security of a free state, the right of people to keep and bear Arms shall not be infringed.'

Second Amendment, US Constitution

'Firearm registration and owner licensing threatens long-standing Canadian liberties and freedoms. The type of gun control Canada has enacted is not consistent with many democratic principles.'

Gary A Mauser, The Fraser Institute, Canada

STATISTICALLY SPEAKING

- 36% of Canadians believe that members of the general public should be allowed to own a gun, and 87% believe that hunters and trapshooters should be allowed to own a gun. Of these, over 90% favoured a mandatory training course, a police background check and a minimum age of 18 for anyone owning a gun. Roughly 60% also favoured a psychological evaluation.

Gallup poll

CONFLICTING EVIDENCE?

The US has a far more tolerant approach to gun ownership than the UK and Australia. Over 35 US states have passed 'right-to-carry' laws enabling licensed gun owners to carry a concealed firearm.

'Right-to-carry states have lower violent crime rates on average: 24% lower total violent crime, 22% lower murder, 37% lower robbery and 20% lower aggravated assault. The five states with the lowest violent crime rates are right-to-carry states.'

National Rifle Association of America

An international comparison of the percentage of violent crimes involving guns

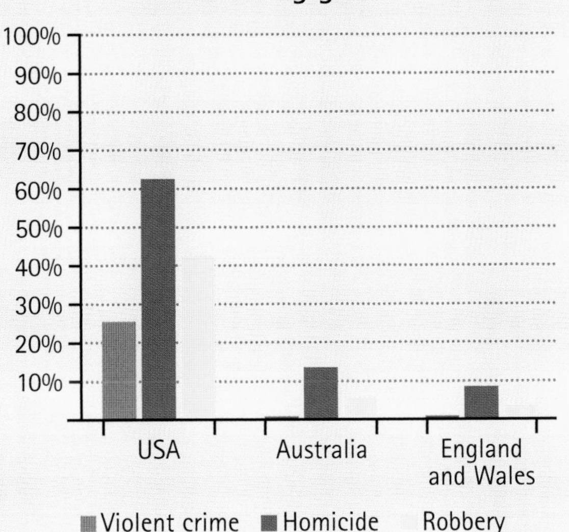

1998–2000 homicide rates per 100,000 population:

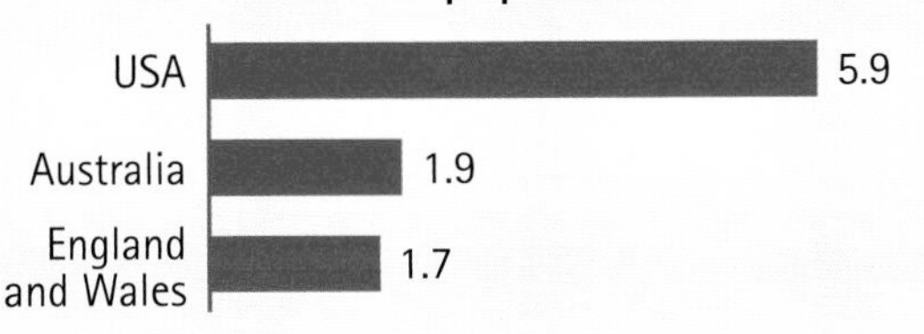

NO 'Ordinary citizens should not have weapons. We do not want the American disease imported into Australia.'

John Howard, Australian Prime Minister

'If future legislation falls short of a complete ban on handguns let all of us be very clear about what we are being told. It says that we and our children are expendable so that 57,000 target shooters can retain their right to pursue a sport that uses weapons designed to kill.'

Anne Pearston, campaigning for a ban on handguns in the UK after the shooting of 16 children and their teacher

'We believe that the availability and lethality of guns make death or severe injury more likely in domestic violence, criminal activity, suicide attempts, and unintentional shootings.'

Belief statement from US gun-control organisation, the Million Mom March

STATISTICALLY SPEAKING

- Approximately 45% of all US households have firearms.
- According to gun-control groups, a British citizen is 50 times less likely to be a victim of gun homicide than an American.

MORE TO THINK ABOUT

This debate has been about the legal ownership of guns. However, most of the world's gun-related crime involves illegal weapons that have been stolen or imported without a licence.

FIND OUT MORE: www.gun-control-network.org www.keepandbeararms.com www.nra.org www.guncontrol.org.au

Q: Should children be treated as adults for serious crimes?

Should juvenile offenders be 'named and shamed' or should their identities be protected by the courts?

IN MANY countries, and for most minor offences, children can be tried in juvenile courts, where their vulnerability and immaturity may be taken into account. Yet juvenile courts are often seen as more lenient than adult courts. Some people believe this is not appropriate for repeat offenders and children convicted of violent crimes. They believe adult courts and long-term sentences should be used. But have a few well-publicised cases inflamed public opinion, or is the juvenile system really failing to protect society from delinquent children?

YES 'This could mean a 17-year-old being sent to the Children's Panel* for beating up his wife ... Delaying effective punishment sends out the wrong message and invites higher crime rates.'

James Douglas-Hamilton, spokesman for the Scottish Conservative Party, commenting about a proposal for Children's Panels to deal with 16- and 17-year-old offenders

* A Children's Panel is a group of unpaid trained volunteers who decide whether compulsory measures of supervision are needed for the child and, if so, what they should be.

'If they commit the crime they should receive adult time.'

Grant McNally, Canadian Alliance MP

'We MUST make serious juvenile offenders responsible as adults, according to their violent crimes.'

Jeanette Basl, 'Fed Up With Crime Committee'

STATISTICALLY SPEAKING

- 23 US states set no minimum age at which children can be tried as adults.

NO

'When I first came to the court, everybody was talking about the "juvenile super-predators", so I kept waiting on the super-predators. They never came. What I saw were 14- and 15-year-olds, scared to death.'

Judge David A Young, Baltimore City, USA

✖ 'Youths differ from adults in their knowledge and experience, time perspective, attitudes towards risk, understanding of alternatives and consequences, and susceptibility to peer-group influences.'

Professor Barry C Feld, University of Minnesota Law School, USA

✖ 'Glib slogans like "Adult time for adult crime" betray the very people that society has failed and encourage "warehousing" of juveniles – in prisons that in reality serve as training grounds for criminals.'

Lisbet Palme, UNICEF

CASE STUDY

THE JAMIE BULGER CASE

In 1993 two 10-year-old boys, Robert Thompson and John Venables, were sentenced to a minimum of eight years in a young offenders institution for the murder of two-year-old Jamie Bulger. One juror at the boys' trial later said the verdict should have been 'guilty as frightened and largely unaware children who made a terrible mistake and are now in urgent need of psychiatric and social help'. The victim's mother said eight years was 'too soon for what they have done'.

STATISTICALLY SPEAKING

- In a study in Florida, USA, children in the adult system were matched by crime and background with children convicted in the juvenile system. It was found that while 30% of children prosecuted in the adult system were re-arrested within 2 years, only 19% of children in the juvenile system were re-arrested.

MORE TO THINK ABOUT

The age of criminal responsibility is the minimum age at which a person can be charged with criminal actions. In India, Ireland, Switzerland, Thailand and most US states this is age 7. In England and Wales it is 10, in Italy and Germany it is 14, in Spain it is 16 and in Luxembourg it is 18. What age do you think it should be? Why?

FIND OUT MORE: www.buildingblocksforyouth.org/issues www.ncjj.org www.youth-justice-board.gov.uk www.lawstuff.org.au

Q: Does community service work better than boot camps?

COMMUNITY SERVICE is sometimes used as an alternative to prison for less serious crimes. The offender must do supervised unpaid work in the community for a set number of hours. Boot camps became popular in the USA in the 1980s and 1990s. The offender is sentenced to a period of 3–4 months in a military-style camp with strong discipline and physical training. However, many argue that it is the elements of education and treatment at such camps that do most to prevent re-offending.

YES

'Doing unpaid labour for 240 hours or any significant number of hours is a deprivation of liberty and is a serious punishment.'

Lord Bingham's (a British judge) view of community service in the UK

'The bullying style and aggressive interactions that characterise the boot camp environment fail to model the pro-social behaviour and development of empathy that these youth really need to learn.'

US National Mental Health Association

'Community sentences aren't about being nice to offenders, they actually work. Offenders must be made to face up to their crimes and pay back to their communities for the harm they have caused.'

Lucie Russell, Director of Smart Justice

NO

'If they are doing community service, say painting someone's fence, they could be staking the place out thinking, "When I've done my community service I will go back there and do that house".'

Lisa Stevens, UK burglary victim speaking on the BBC 'Today' programme

'We should take 12 to 15 year olds out of the neighbourhoods in which they are causing the problem and into secure training ... You send out the message to the person's peer group that you don't come back laughing from the courts.'

Ann Widdecombe, British Member of Parliament

'Kids can't be mollycoddled by the do-gooders of today; it doesn't do them any good. They have to learn discipline. And if they don't learn to fend for themselves, they've had it.'

Ron Lovelock, who spent two years in a secure home for delinquent boys in the 1960s

A shock programme for inmates at a prison in Florida, USA.

Sample regime at a young offender institution

06:00 Rise, clean room, drill
06:40 Room inspection
07:20 Drill
08:00 Breakfast
08:30 Skills training, education
12:00 Lunch
13:00 Physical education
14:15 Skills training, education
16:45 Personal hygiene
17:00 Evening meal
18:00 Drama, art, drugs awareness
20:00 Group meeting
20:30 Earned privileges
21:45 Personal hygiene

STATISTICALLY SPEAKING

Victims of Crime survey
Percentage of victims preferring a community service sentence for young repeat-offending burglars

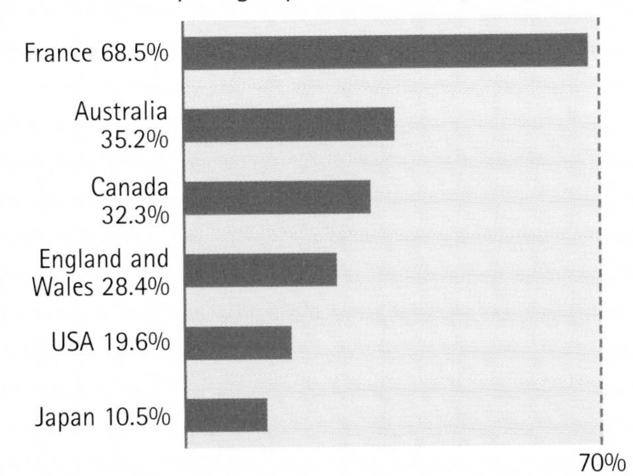

STATISTICALLY SPEAKING

- Re-offending rates at US boot camps average between 64% and 75%. This is close to the re-offending rates at traditional correctional institutions.

MORE TO THINK ABOUT

'Community service' was officially renamed 'community punishment' in the UK in 2002. Why do you think the government decided on this change of title?

Q: Are the police doing enough to tackle car crime?

Some people say car crime is 'victimless' because insurance companies pay for the loss. However, car owners have to pay higher insurance to cover the cost.

CAR CRIME is one of the most common types of crime. It includes vandalism, theft from a car, or theft of the car itself. A high proportion of offenders are either young 'joy-riders' or opportunistic thieves who see an unlocked door or a purse on a car seat. They often commit multiple offences before they are caught. Police initiatives tend to focus on raising public awareness about basic car security, and catching the professional car thief who steals a car for re-sale or parts.

YES

'It must be remembered that the responsibility lies with users and owners to reduce the risk of crimes being committed on their cars.'

Department of Police and Public Safety, Tasmania, Australia

'Car crime is a policing priority. [We use] a mixture of intelligence-led policing, pro-active work and forensic analysis to catch and convict car thieves.'

Essex Police reporting the launch of the UK's first 'decoy car'

'Car thieves should watch out. We are constantly receiving information on their activities and we will target anyone we believe is active in this type of crime.'

Detective Inspector Kevin Mills, Sheffield, UK

'I think [joy-riding] is a community problem ... I'd ask the community what they are doing about it and ask the parents what are their responsibilities.'

Acting Assistant Commissioner Bob Hastings of the Melbourne Police, commenting after a joy-riding incident involving ten teenagers.

NO 'Car crime has reached epidemic levels in Northern Ireland. Both the police and the courts could begin by taking a more strident line ... in sentencing those so-called "joy-riders" who frequently deal in death on our roads.'

William McCrea, Democratic Unionist spokesman, Northern Ireland

✖ 'I have watched as youths stole my neighbour's car in broad daylight – when I phoned the police they said it was a "low priority" incident.'

Participant in the BBC Online 'Talking Point'

✖ 'Over the past few years, a proportion of police resources once allocated to fight vehicle theft has been reallocated to fighting crimes against the person. Because most stolen vehicles are replaced by insurance, the crime of vehicle theft is often perceived to be a "victimless" one.'

Insurance Bureau of Canada

STATISTICALLY SPEAKING

- According to the Australian Institute of Criminology, the average car thief steals a car 47 times before recording a conviction.
- 45% of victims of car crime report incidents to the police but just one in 10 expect anyone to be charged, according to one 2004 survey.

(Autoglass *Cracking Crime* Report)

MORE TO THINK ABOUT

Only about 14% of car thefts are cleared by arrests in the USA. The FBI says this is because of 'the nature of the crime, its volume, and the degree of difficulty in solving this particular crime'. Do they have a point?

Leaving your vehicle's engine running when nobody is in it is illegal in Pennsylvania, USA. The idea is to deter opportunistic car thieves. But is it fair to vehicle owners?

FIND OUT MORE: www.racfoundation.org www.watchyourcar.org www.crimereduction.gov.uk/toolkits www.carsafe.com.au

Q: Do violent video games lead to violent crime?

The overwhelming majority of children who play 'first person shooter' games do not commit violent acts.

MANY PEOPLE believe instinctively that 'first person shooter' games in which the player participates in graphic screen violence must lead to increased aggression. Studies show that such games lead to short-term increases in aggressive activity amongst young children, but the evidence for older children and adults is less clear. Some argue that violent games can actually reduce violent tendencies by releasing aggression in a harmless way.

YES 'High levels of violent video game exposure have been linked to delinquency, fighting at school and violent criminal behaviour.'

Professor Craig Anderson, Iowa State University, USA

'These games send kids the message that violence is acceptable, exciting and without consequence.'

Mary Lou Dickerson, US State Representative and mother of two

'We are raising the risk that more people will be inclined to use violence when put into a conflict situation and they're more likely to become desensitised to the use of violence by other people.'

Barbara Biggins, Young Media Australia

STATISTICALLY SPEAKING

• People in the USA and Japan have arguably similar rates of participation in violent video games. Yet Japan's murder rate is around 800 per year in a population of 127 million while in New York, the murder rate is around 600 per year in a population of just 8 million.

CASE STUDY

WARREN LEBLANC

Warren Leblanc, 17, murdered 14-year-old Stefan Pakeerah after luring him to a park. Stefan's family believe that Leblanc was acting out an adult-rated video game called Manhunt, which had already been banned in some countries. Stefan's father said, 'The way Warren committed the murder is how the game is set out – killing people using weapons like hammers and knives. There is some connection between the game and what he has done.'

Industry response

A spokesman for the video games industry said, 'simply being in someone's possession does not and should not lead to the conclusion that a game is responsible for these tragic events' and the police found no connection between the murder and Manhunt. Nevertheless, some retailers did remove the adult-rated game from their shelves.

NO

'Youth violence in America has fallen dramatically over the precise time period that video games have skyrocketed.'

Neil Seeman, Canadian lawyer and health care researcher

✖ 'While video games may provide a simple excuse for the teenagers involved in this incident, responsibility for violent acts belongs to those who commit them.'

Douglas Lowenstein, games industry spokesman, commenting on claims by teenage boys that they were acting out the Grand Theft Auto game when they shot at passing vehicles in Tennessee, USA

✖ 'I've played the Mortal Kombat game – you know it's violent but it's sort of funny ... the way they chop their heads off. You just laugh because it's so funny 'cos you know it's not real.'

Female respondent, 15–17 years, Computer Games and Australians Today project

STATISTICALLY SPEAKING

• One study has calculated that by the time typical American children reach the age of 18, they have seen 200,000 acts of violence and 40,000 murders on some sort of screen.

MORE TO THINK ABOUT

There is, as yet, no firm evidence that playing violent video games increases violent behaviour. Many studies have found a link between the two, but this may be because those with existing aggressive tendencies are more likely to play violent video games.

Q: Can drunkenness ever be an excuse for crime?

MOST ADULTS who drink alcohol excessively do so without committing any sort of crime. However, it is accepted that there is a link between drunkenness and crime. Offences ranging from anti-social behaviour to dangerous driving, assault and murder are more likely to occur where alcohol is involved. Defendants frequently argue that they were drunk and not therefore responsible for their own actions. However, others argue that drinking large amounts of alcohol is a choice, not an excuse.

NO

'The statistics show a direct causal link between alcohol and the increase in reported violent crimes. Many people nowadays don't go out for a drink – they go out to get drunk.'

Mrs Jan Berry, Chair of the Police Federation of England and Wales

'Drinking and driving is a choice. It's a violent crime.'

Millie Webb, victim of drunk driving and US spokeswoman for Mothers Against Drunk Driving

'[Drunkenness] should be viewed as an aggravating, not a mitigating circumstance ... A world in which having been a drunken member of an angry mob can protect against the legal consequences of murder is one in which we all have reason to feel profound unease.'

Theodore Dalrymple, US columnist

Danish police remove a drunk man from a town centre.

YES 'While drunkenness is not normally an excuse or mitigating factor, where the abuse of alcohol ... reflects the socio-economic circumstances and environment in which the offender has grown up, that can and should be taken into account as a mitigating factor.'

Sentencing guidelines with regard to members of Aboriginal communities, Supreme Court of New South Wales

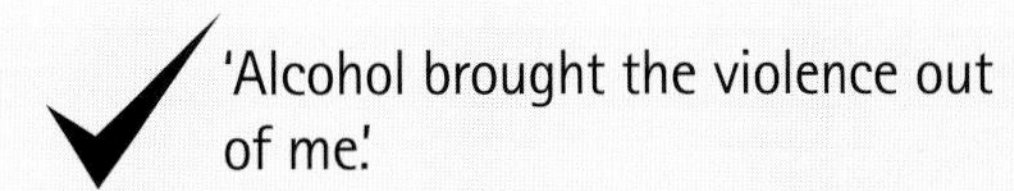

'Alcohol brought the violence out of me.'

Quote from a man who attacked his wife in Michigan, USA

'Alcopops have an alcoholic content higher than that of most beers and lagers but with strong flavours like vanilla or lemonade. It is quite possible to drink such a product without realising its true content.'

Dr Garry Slapper, Staffordshire University, UK

CASE STUDY

DRINK DRIVING

Most countries disallow driving at prescribed levels (measured as Blood Alcohol Content or BAC), but these levels vary both by country and by situation. However there is no foolproof guide to how much alcohol you can drink and still stay within the law. It depends on the type of alcohol you have drunk, how much you weigh, your sex, age and metabolism.

Level at which a driver is legally intoxicated by country:

Sweden: 0.02%

Australia: 0.05%

Netherlands: 0.05%

UK: 0.08%

USA: 0.08%

STATISTICALLY SPEAKING

- Those most likely to mix motoring and alcohol are males aged between 17 and 29.

STATISTICALLY SPEAKING

- Alcohol is present in more than 50% of all incidents of domestic violence, according to the US Department of Health and Human Services.
- A survey in the UK found that 39% of 'binge drinkers' (those who got very drunk at least once a month) aged 18-24 reported committing an offence in the previous 12 months, compared to 14% of regular drinkers.

MORE TO THINK ABOUT

A French couple who allowed a friend to drive home after a drunken dinner party at their house went on trial charged with being partially responsible for the car crash in which he killed himself and four others. They were acquitted (found not guilty). Was this a reasonable outcome, in your view?

FIND OUT MORE: www.alcoholconcern.org.uk www.madd.org www.crimereduction.gov.uk/drugsalcohol8 www.drugwarfacts.org/alcohol.htm

Q: Are black people treated unfairly by the justice system?

MANY COUNTRIES with a mainly white population send a disproportionately high number of black people to prison. Black people also tend to be under-represented on juries, in the police and amongst lawyers and judges. Some argue that this is because the police are prejudiced, or the courts are discriminatory. Others argue that black people are more likely to experience deprivation or dislocation which increases their likelihood of committing a crime.

YES 'Aboriginal people are grossly over-represented at all points of contact with the criminal justice system (except in regard to staffing and access to victim services wherein they are grossly under-represented).'

Western Australian Aboriginal Justice Agreement

✔ '"Are we impartial here?" is a question that arises when a person of colour looks across the courtroom to see an all-white jury.'

Pennsylvania Supreme Court Committee Report on Racial and Gender Bias in the Justice System

✔ 'Racial discrimination in the contemporary US legal system remains deeply ingrained.'

Amnesty International

STATISTICALLY SPEAKING

- Out of 714,000 stops and searches by UK police in 2002, 12% were of black people, who make up 1.8% of the total population.

NO 'I don't see it.'

The response of Rhode Island Supreme Court Chief Justice Frank Williams when asked if there was any racial discrimination in US State courts

✘ 'I'm a police officer and all I'm trying to do is a good job and prevent crime. I get sick of hearing people complain when I stop them that it's because they're black and I have no reason to.'

Clive, BBC Online 'Talking Point'

STATISTICALLY SPEAKING

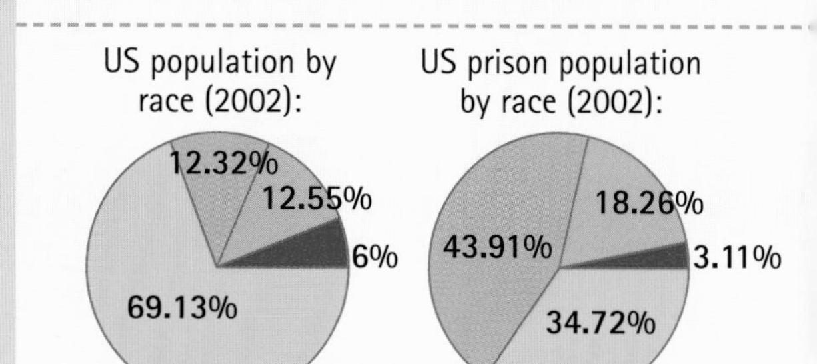

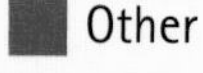

CASE STUDY

STEPHEN LAWRENCE

Stephen Lawrence was murdered in London in 1993. No one has been convicted of his murder, but his parents and many campaigners believe he was the victim of a racist attack.

Doreen Lawrence, mother of Stephen, said, 'My son was stereotyped by the police: he was black, then he must be a criminal. [His] crime was that he was walking down the road looking for a bus to take him home. Our crime is living in a country where the justice system supports racist murderers against innocent people.'

After the murder, many people accused London's police force of ineptitude, complacency and even racism in the way they conducted the investigation. A public inquiry was held in 1998, and the report concluded that the treatment of the Lawrence family and the police investigation itself were marred by 'institutional racism' within the police force.

Nevertheless, the report also said, 'We have heard no evidence of overt racism or discrimination [within the police], unless it can be said that the use of inappropriate expressions such as "coloured" or "negro" fall into that category.'

STATISTICALLY SPEAKING

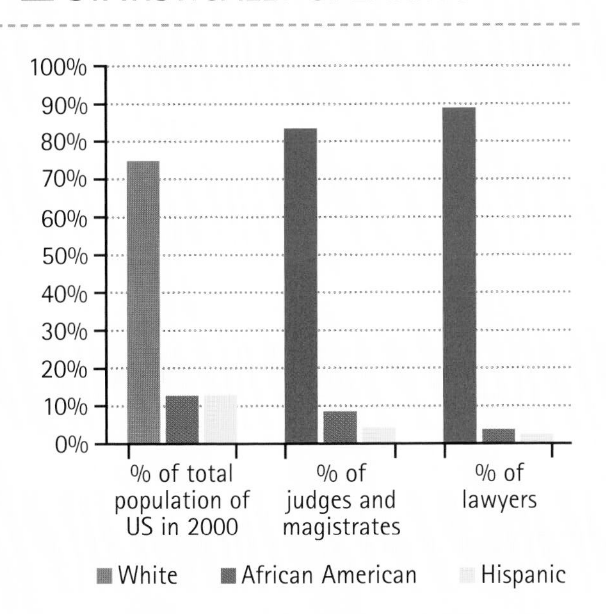

MORE TO THINK ABOUT

The Canadian Criminal Code directs judges to consider non-custodial sentences wherever possible, 'with particular attention to the circumstances of aboriginal offenders'. Is it appropriate to use positive discrimination, sometimes known as 'affirmative action' to try to reverse the high proportion of aboriginal or black inmates in our prisons today?

FIND OUT MORE: www.buildingblocksforyouth.org www.cre.gov.uk www.racismnoway.com.au www.hrw.org/campaigns/race/criminal_justice.htm

Q: Should drugs be legalised?

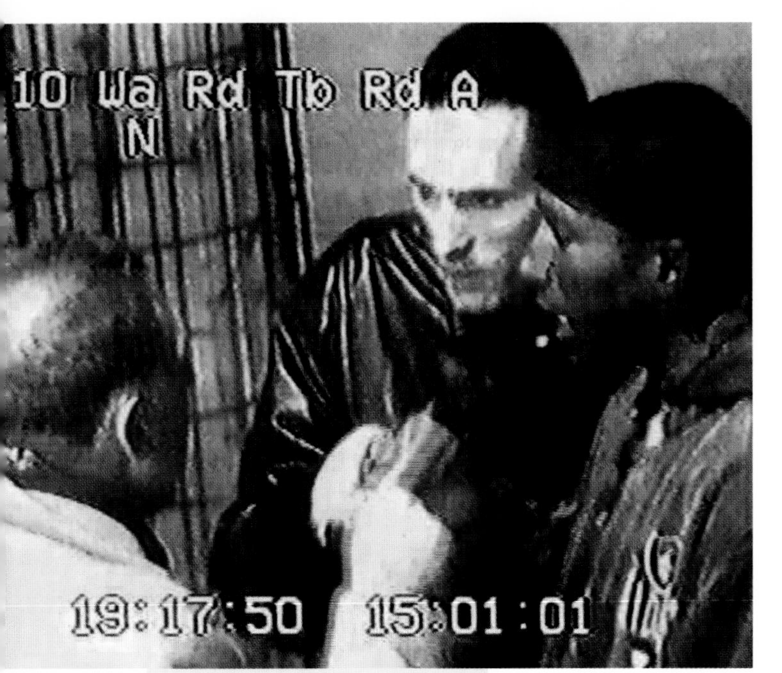

Two drug dealers are caught selling crack cocaine by a hidden police camera.

IN MOST countries the possession or sale of drugs such as cannabis, cocaine and heroin is a criminal offence. Many believe that legalisation would lead to an increase in addiction. However, others argue that the 'war on drugs' is not working. They say that illegal drugs encourage smugglers and dealers, while addicts are forced into crime to pay for their habit. Cannabis is the most widely used illegal drug but unlike 'hard' drugs such as heroin it is not physically addictive. For this reason, some campaigners believe cannabis alone should be legalised, enabling the police to focus on more 'serious' crimes.

YES 'The drugs war is unwinnable, costly and counterproductive ... Colombia saw a dramatic increase in violence and corruption as prohibition made cocaine a profitable commodity.'

Sir Keith Morris, former UK ambassador to Colombia

'If there had been a controlled environment for my son to take his heroin, and it had been supplied legally, he would still be alive.'

Fulton Gillespie, whose son died after taking heroin which contained impurities

'Drug prohibition turns otherwise law-abiding citizens into criminals and fuels crime at all levels.'

Transform Drug Policy Foundation

STATISTICALLY SPEAKING

- 'Treatment has been shown to be 7.3 times more effective than law enforcement in reducing the drug problem and related problems such as crime.'

Australian campaign group Families and Friends for Drug Law Reform

NO

'The legalisation of drugs would make harmful and addictive substances affordable, available, convenient, and marketable. It would expand the use of drugs ... and remove the social stigma attached to illegal drug use.'

Drug Watch International

'To discourage the use of illegal drugs and to deter the damaging personal and economic effects of all types of drug use, individuals convicted of illegal drug offences should be punished to the fullest extent prescribed by law.'

George W Bush, US President

'The state must not assist its most vulnerable citizens to alienate themselves from society and ruin their lives.'

Catholic Archbishop Giuseppe Lazzarotto speaking against the legalisation of drugs

'We'd make sure the drug traffickers have only two places to stay – jail or the cemetery.'

Thaksin Shinawatra, Prime Minister of Thailand

CONFLICTING EVIDENCE?

'There are very few young heroin addicts in the Netherlands, largely thanks to the policy of separating the user markets for hard and soft drugs. The number of addicts ... has been stable for many years.'

Netherlands Ministry of Justice

'Since the legalisation of marijuana in the Netherlands, heroin addiction levels have tripled.'

US Drug Enforcement Agency

STATISTICALLY SPEAKING

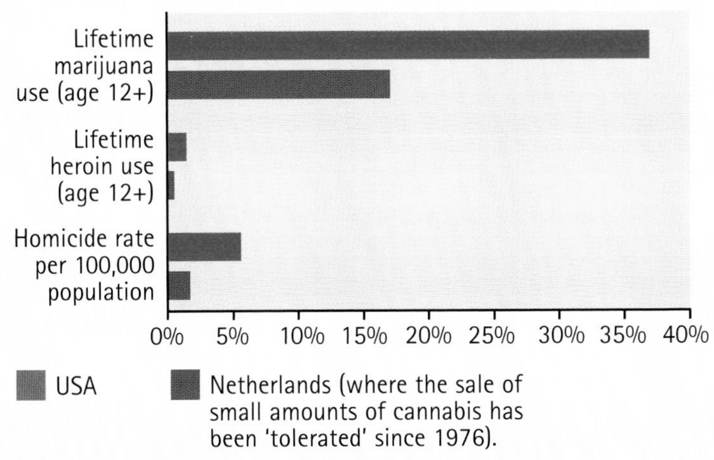

Source: various, compiled by Drug War Facts

MORE TO THINK ABOUT

The debate about drugs involves a number of issues not covered here. These include: the costs to society of enforcing drug laws; civil liberties; alcohol and nicotine as legal drugs; and whether cannabis has any health benefits, particularly for sufferers of multiple sclerosis.

FIND OUT MORE: www.DrugWarFacts.org www.tdpf.org.uk www.drugprevent.demon.co.uk www.drugwatch.org www.ffdlr.org.au

Q: Is downloading music from the Internet the same as shoplifting?

MOST MUSIC, movies and books are protected by copyright. This means that their creators, or 'owners' have exclusive rights to copy and communicate their works to the public. Despite such laws, the music industry sees a growing threat from individuals who download music from unauthorised sites on the Internet. Because the copyright owner is not paid, many argue that this is the same as theft. However, others believe that copyright is an outdated law, and that unrestricted downloading benefits everyone, including the music industry.

NO

'Researchers believe that most downloading is done by teens and college kids, groups that are "money-poor but time-rich", meaning they wouldn't have bought the songs they downloaded. In that sense, the music industry can't claim those downloads as lost sales.'

Sean Silverthorne, Editor, Harvard Business School journal

'The Internet is just one huge word of mouth. The more an artist is heard, the more likely people will go out and purchase the album legally.'

High School student, Port Washington, New York, USA

'The culture has shifted. It's not about buying music anymore. If the industry doesn't respond quickly, it's going to be in big trouble. We can't shut these people down.'

Russell Simmons, co-founder of Def Jam Records

YES

'It's the same thing as going into a CD store and stealing the CD.'

Britney Spears, singer

'Most songwriters are not rich or famous. They are hardworking craftsmen who depend on their royalties to provide for their children. Stealing music is stealing from their families.'

Matraca Berg, songwriter

'Whatever any of us feel about the price of anything, that doesn't justify stealing. Illegal file-sharing is theft under copyright law.'

David Munns, vice-chairman of EMI Music

If you copy or distribute copyrighted music without permission, you can be prosecuted in a criminal court and sued for damages in a civil court.

STATISTICALLY SPEAKING

Percentage of Australia's population who agree that downloading unauthorised music from the Internet is like stealing from a record store

(Source: 2003 survey for the Australian Record Industry Association)

CONFLICTING EVIDENCE?

Amongst Internet-connected music consumers, those who say they are downloading more also say they are purchasing less by a margin of over two to one.

Recording Industry Association of America

A study comparing music downloads with album sales showed that while the number of illegal downloads continued to increase, so did music sales.

Professor Felix Oberholzer-Gee and Koleman Strumpf, USA

MORE TO THINK ABOUT

It is perfectly legal to download music from sites authorised by the owners of the copyrighted music, whether or not such sites charge a fee. It is illegal to download music from unauthorised sites or file-sharing 'peer-to-peer' systems. It is also illegal to make unauthorised copies of music available to others through file sharing or CD burning. However, if you are unsure of the law, check first.

FIND OUT MORE: www.musicunited.org www.bpi.co.uk www.pro-music.org www.fact-uk.org.uk

Q: Should victims' rights be more important than defendants' rights?

MANY PEOPLE believe that the justice system is unfairly weighted in the defendant's favour. Victims of crime often feel overlooked by the courts, and some think that a defendant's previous convictions should be made known to the jury to avoid guilty people walking free. However, the principle of 'innocent until proven guilty' is enshrined in the justice systems of many countries and the courts have to be extremely careful not to prejudice the outcome of trials.

YES

'Far too many of the nearly 25 million Americans who become victims of crime each year must struggle on their own with the enormous emotional, financial and physical consequences of crime ... We must do more than merely tinker with offender-oriented systems that are not designed to address victims' needs.'

Susan Herman, National Center for Victims of Crime, USA

'This measure ... is designed to make it clear we are not going to have people playing the system and getting away with criminal offences that cause real misery to ordinary citizens.'

British Prime Minister Tony Blair, talking about a change in the law to allow juries to hear about a defendant's previous convictions

'The Victim Impact Statement is your opportunity to tell the court about the impact the crime has had on you. It is a factor that the court will take into account in sentencing. It may help the defendant realise the effects of what he or she has done.'

Government of South Australia

NO

'Telling juries about [previous convictions] may get the result the government wants – more convictions – but far too many of them will be the wrongful convictions of innocent people.'

John Wadham, director of human rights organisation, Liberty

'Society must separate contempt for his act from respect for his right.'

The Israeli Supreme Court, upholding the right of prisoners to vote

'Everyone charged with a penal offence has the right to be presumed innocent until proven guilty according to law in a public trial at which he has all the guarantees necessary for his defence.'

Article 11, UN Declaration of Human Rights

CASE STUDY

RESTORATIVE JUSTICE

Restorative Justice is the name given to the process of repairing the harm caused by crime. Victims, offenders and affected members of the community are brought together by a court-appointed mediator. The idea is that offenders recognise the impact of what they have done and make amends, and victims have their harm or loss acknowledged. It is not generally intended as a substitute for punishment.

Results

Some studies report high levels of satisfaction with the process, but figures for the re-offending rates of participants are scarce and it does depend on the offender pleading guilty before the process can begin. A UK Home Office report in 2005 found that 'restorative cautioning', in which offenders apologise to their victims, had little effect on reconviction rates.

Damian Divine (left), a reformed offender, said his outlook had changed since he was faced with the parents of his 15-year-old victim. He said, 'From my point of view bringing the parents round made me realise that it had an effect on someone.'

STATISTICALLY SPEAKING

- Over 50,000 people in the UK are imprisoned each year awaiting trial. When they finally stand trial, one in five are acquitted (not guilty).

Source: Prison Reform Trust

An ICM poll in the UK asked members of the public whether they thought a jury should know about a defendant's previous criminal record before they consider their verdict

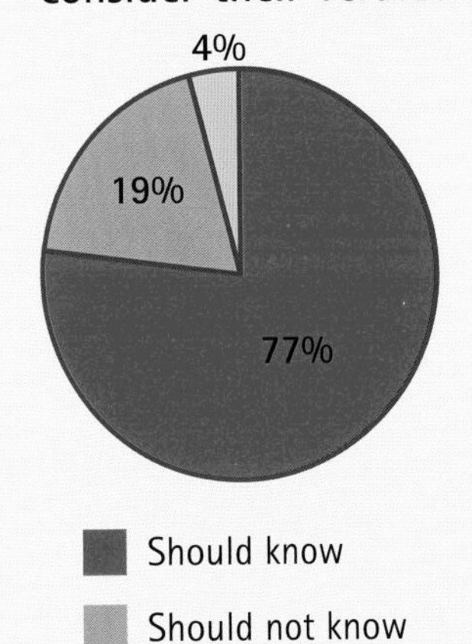

MORE TO THINK ABOUT

There are many issues to do with balancing the rights of the victim and the defendant that have not been mentioned here. These include: compensation for victims, early release of offenders from prison and terrorist suspects imprisoned indefinitely without trial.

FIND OUT MORE: www.ncvc.org www.innocentuntilprovenguilty.com www.victimsofcrime.org.uk www.voc.sa.gov.au www.liberty-human-rights.org.uk

Q: Should euthanasia be treated as unlawful killing?

'VOLUNTARY EUTHANASIA' means receiving help in order to die. This 'help' may mean supplying drugs, administering a lethal injection, giving information about how the drugs might be obtained or not intervening to prevent such a death. In most countries euthanasia is treated as unlawful killing, or even murder. However, in the Netherlands, Belgium and in Oregon, USA 'assisted suicide' for people who are terminally ill is legal in some circumstances.

YES

'If you see someone standing on a bridge considering suicide you don't push them off. Euthanasia is giving them that push.'

Spokeswoman for the Pro-Life Alliance

'Once the power to kill is bestowed on physicians ... a patient can no longer be sure what role the doctor will play – healer or killer.'

International Task Force on Euthanasia and Assisted Suicide

'[Euthanasia could] potentially create an open season for the killing of disabled people.'

Tara Flood, UK Disability Awareness in Action

NO

'This is the trial of everyone who's ever made a promise that they would help someone die gently if necessary, and the trial of every doctor who has helped and remained silent.'

Lesley Martin speaking at her trial in New Zealand. Martin had given her terminally-ill mother an overdose of morphine. She was convicted of attempted murder and jailed for 15 months

'The patient always makes the last act – swallowing the drug or opening a valve of a drip himself – so we never had a problem with the police.'

Ludwig Minelli, director of Dignitas, a Swiss charity that helps terminally ill people die

'The law produces the apparently irrational result that people can choose to die lingering deaths by refusing treatment that keeps them alive ... but they cannot choose a quick, painless death that their doctors could easily provide.'

Professor Ronald Dworkin, University College, London

STATISTICALLY SPEAKING

- A poll of disabled people in the UK found that 80% would back a bill allowing a rational disabled person with a terminal disease to be helped to die.

CONFLICTING EVIDENCE?

Does legislation mean more deaths?

According to the Netherlands law, doctors involved in voluntary euthanasia must:

- be convinced that the patient's request is voluntary, well-considered and lasting;
- be convinced that the patient's suffering is unbearable and unremitting;
- have reached the conclusion with the patient that there is no reasonable alternative.

Percentage of all deaths in Australia and the Netherlands, 1995

	Australia No legal euthanasia	Netherlands Limited euthanasia permitted
Voluntary euthanasia	1.7%	2.4%
Physician assisted suicide	0.1%	0.3%
Ending life without explicit request	3.5%	0.7%
Withholding life prolonging treatment	28.6%	20.2%
Pain relief likely to hasten death	30.9%	19.1%
Total	64.8%	42.7%

In the Netherlands in 2001 it was estimated that doctors ended the lives of 840 people without their specific request. In a recent survey, 10% of Dutch senior citizens said they feared being killed by their doctor without their consent.

MORE TO THINK ABOUT

This debate has focused on the assisted deaths of older people who are terminally ill. However, the Netherlands is currently considering legislation on the assisted deaths of terminally ill babies and children and people who are mentally incapacitated. Is this the 'slippery slope' that anti-euthanasia campaigners fear?

Dr Jack Kevorkian was known as 'Dr Death' for his role in over 100 assisted suicides in the USA. In 1999 he was convicted of second-degree murder for giving a lethal injection to a terminally ill patient who had requested it. He received a minimum 10-year prison sentence.

FIND OUT MORE: www.qrtl.org.au www.nvve.nl www.ves.org.uk. www.euthanasia.com

Glossary

Aboriginal people who are native to a country – their ancestors have inhabited a region from the beginning.

Alcopops drinks with a strong alcoholic base mixed with sweet or fruit flavours.

Anti-social behaviour includes a wide range of problems such as noisy neighbours, graffiti, litter and public nuisance.

Arson the criminal act of deliberately setting fire to something.

Biometric data any unique physical characteristic such as an iris scan or thumbprint by which a person can be identified.

Cannabis a mood-altering drug from the cannabis plant, which is usually smoked. It is illegal in many countries.

Capital punishment the death penalty – the killing of a prisoner for a crime such as murder.

Copyright the law which gives exclusive rights to someone to copy and communicate their original works to the public.

Cyber crime crime conducted electronically via the Internet.

Death Row where prisoners who have been sentenced to death await their sentence.

Defendant person accused of a crime in court.

Delinquent a young person who has a tendency to commit crime.

Deprivation hardship such as homelessness or poverty.

Deterrent a punishment that acts as a warning to others.

Discrimination treating someone unfairly because they are different (e.g. different colour, sex, religion).

Download to transfer data, such as music, from a server, such as the Internet, or host computer to your own computer.

Euthanasia bringing about an easy death; assisted suicide.

Exclusion barred because of bad behaviour (e.g. from school).

Forensic chemical evidence such as DNA or soil particles that may be used in a court of law.

Heroin a highly-addictive illegal drug extracted from the Asian poppy.

Homicide unlawful killing.

Identity fraud To use the identity of a person without their consent, for a purpose that the person is not aware of, generally for an illegal activity, such as theft with credit cards.

Illegal immigrant someone who moves to another country without permission.

Impartial fair, without prejudice or favour.

Incarceration imprisonment.

Joy-rider person who has stolen a car in order to drive it for fun, probably recklessly.

Juror a member of the public who has been chosen to sit on a jury at a trial.

Juvenile a child or young person not yet adult in the eyes of the law.

Legislation a law, or laws, that has been proposed or is already in force in a country.

Liberal someone who does not take a hard line; accepting a broad range of viewpoints.

Mentally incapacitated unable to make a rational decision or take responsibility for one's actions.

Mitigating factor something that may lessen a person's responsibility for a crime (e.g. mental illness).

Non-custodial sentence punishment that does not involve a prison sentence (e.g. a Community Service Order).

Offender someone who has been convicted of a crime.

Penal offence offence punishable by law.

Prejudice a judgement formed beforehand or without knowledge of the facts. Prejudice is sometimes an irrational suspicion or hatred of a particular group, race, or religion.

Premeditated an act that has been planned or considered beforehand.

Prohibition a law forbidding the sale of something such as drugs or alcohol.

Racism hatred of or prejudice against someone because of their race.

Rehabilitation help and support for an offender to stop them from re-offending.

Restorative justice a process where an offender meets his or her victim to apologise or make amends.

Retroactively after the fact.

Terminally ill dying.

Terrorist someone who carries out a serious criminal act, often against innocent victims, to draw attention to their cause.

Unanimous in complete agreement.

Verdict the decision of a judge or a jury at the end of a trial.

White-collar crime crime against business – often fraud or embezzlement.

Witness someone who sees an event and reports what happened, possibly in a court of law.

Zero-tolerance the policy of pursuing every criminal, however small their crime.

Debating tips

WHAT IS DEBATING?

A debate is a structured argument. Two teams speak in turn for or against a particular question. Usually each person is given a time they are allowed to speak for and any remarks from the other side are controlled. The subject of the debate is often already decided so you may find yourself having to support opinions with which you might not agree. You may also have to argue as part of a team, being careful not to contradict what others on your side have said.

After both sides have had their say, and had a chance to answer the opposition, the audience votes on which side they agree with.

DEBATING SKILLS

1 Know your subject

Research it as much as you can. The debates in this book give opinions as a starting point, but there are website suggestions for you to find out more. Use facts and information to support your points.

2 Make notes

Write down key words and phrases on cards. Try not to read a prepared speech. You might end up losing your way and stuttering.

3 Watch the time

You may be given a set amount of time for your presentation, so stick to it.

4 Practise how you sound

Try to sound natural. Think about:
Speed – Speak clearly and steadily. Try to talk at a pace that is fast enough to sound intelligent and allows you time to say what you want, but slow enough to be understood.
Tone – Varying the tone of your voice will make you sound interesting.
Volume – Speak at a level at which everyone in the room can comfortably hear you. Shouting does not win debates. Variation of volume (particularly speaking more quietly at certain points) can help you to emphasise important points but the audience must still be able to hear you.
Don't ramble – Short, clear sentences work well and are easier to understand.

GET INVOLVED - NATIONAL DEBATING LEAGUES

Worldwide links
www.debating.net

Debating Matters, UK
www.debatingmatters.com

Auckland Debating Society, New Zealand
www.ada.org.nz/schlevels.php

Debaters Association of Victoria, Australia
www.debating.netspace.net.au

Index

Acknowledgements

Picture credits: © Corbis Sygma: 21. © Lou Dematteis/ Reuters/Corbis: 11. © Najlah Feanny/Corbis Saba: 22. © Brownie Harris/Corbis: 28. © Himmel Lizzie/Corbis: 12. © Reuters/Corbis: 6. © Fatih Saribas/Reuters/Corbis: 14. © Steve Starr/Corbis: cover, 27. © Pidgeon Thomas/Corbis Sygma: 43. © David Woods/Corbis: 24. Tim Ockenden/PA/Empics: 41. Laurence Cendrowicz/Franklin Watts: 25, 29. Chris Fairclough/Franklin Watts: 10. Rex Features: 4-5, 16, 18, 35. Francis Dean/Rex Features: 32. Isopress/Rex Features: 30. Mark St. George/Rex Features: 36. Keystone/TopFoto: 38-39. Novosti/TopFoto: 8.

Text credits: P6: 1 Vic Bilson, 'Death in the School Yard': http://www.jeremiahproject.com/prophecy/schoolyard.html (01/07/05); 2 Anon, 2005; 3 Joschka Fischer quoted in 'Cybercrime' by Peter Gould and Chris Summers, January 2001: http://news.bbc.co.uk/hi/english/static/in_depth/uk/2001/life_of_crime/cybercrime.stm (01/07/05). P7: 1 Don Weatherburn quoted in 'NSW crime figures dip for a third year', 23 Aug 2004: http://www.bananas-in-pyjamas.com.au/nsw/news/200408/s1182801.htm (01/07/05); 2 Rosemary Gartner, 1998 ; 3 Vincent Schiraldi, 1998. P8: 1 Richar Burr, 'A Child On Death Row, A Tragedy Unfolding': http://www.ccadp.org/grahamchild.htm (01/07/05); 2 Daljeet Dagon quoted in 'There are no silver spoons for children born into poverty', Barnado's, 2003: http://www.barnardos.org.uk/newsandevents/media/resource/REPORT.PDF (01/07/05); 3 Lisbet Palme, 'No age of innocence: Justice for children', 1997: http://www.unicef.org/pon97/protec1b.htm (01/07/05). Page 9: 1 Dan quoted in 'Is crime being tackled properly?' BBC online talking point, 2003: http://news.bbc.co.uk/1/hi/talking_point/3106369.stm (01/07/05); 2 Catholic bishops of New Zealand, 'Creating New Hearts: Moving From Retributive to Restorative Justice', 30 Aug 1995: http://www.ccjc.ca/currentissues/newzealand.cfm (01/07/05); 3 Haney, C, 'The Social Context of Capital Murder: Social Histories and the Logic of Mitigation', *Santa Clara Law Review 547* quoting Decision, In the Matter of the Clemency Request of Robert Alton Harris, (16 Apr 1992). P10: 1 Nicole Billante, 'The Beat Goes On: Policing for Crime Prevention', Centre for Independent Studies, 1 July 2003; 2 Maureen Brookes quoted in *The Observer*, 27 Nov 2004; 3 Sarah Teather quoted in *North West London Newspapers*, 3 Nov 2004, 4 Slogan on Conservative Party campaign poster, UK, 2005. P11: 1 Zaki Hashmi, BBC Talking Point, 12 July, 2002: http://news.bbc.co.uk/1/low/talking_point/forum/2118682.stm (01/07/05); 2 Tim Anderson, 'Zero tolerance' policing – a big lie', 1998: http://www.greenleft.org.au/back/1998/326/326p14b.htm (01/07/05). P12: 1 Stephen P Bohrer quoted in *San Francisco Chronicle*, 1 Dec 2001, 2 South Australia Department of Correctional Services, 'Illicit Drugs and Correctional Services', June 2002; 3 Professor Paul Robinson quoted in *Penn News*, 22 Apr 2004. P13: 1 Annabel Goldie, Press Release – Scottish Conservatives, 24 Feb 2004; 2 US Deputy Attorney General Larry Thompson – Press Release, Jan 2003; 3 David Green quoted in *The Times* (London), 12 May 2004; 4 Levi's story: reproduced with permission of Prison Me No-Way!; P14: 1 David Blunkett, speech to the Institute of Public Policy Research, 17 Nov 2004; 2 Mrs Jan Berry – Press release, 23 Nov 2004; 3 Clive Williams quoted in *The Canberra Times*, 16 Oct 2003. P15: 1 American Civil Liberties Union, 5 Problems with National ID Cards', 8 Sep 2003: http://www.aclu.org/news/NewsPrint.cfm?ID=13501&c=39 (01/07/05); 2 Adrian Beck from pamphlet 'Id Cards: Arguments Against', *Liberty and Charter 88*, Dec 2002; 3 Simon Davies, 'In Search of Perfect Identity', *The International Privacy Bulletin*, Vol. 4, No. 2, Spring 1996. P16: 1 Hu Jintao quoted in *Legal Daily*, 4 May 1996; 2 Vikki Haack quoted in 'Many grieving families seek comfort and closure in the execution of the murderer. Do they find it?' *US News & World Report* , 17 June 1997; 3 John McAdams: prodeathpenalty.com (01/07/05). P17: 1 Amnesty: http://web.amnesty.org/library/index/engasa170032004 (01/07/05); 2 Albert Pierrepoint, *Executioner: Pierrepoint*, Harrap, 1974; 3 US Congress Subcommittee on Civil and Constitutional Rights, Staff report, 1993; 4 Hasham Dezhbakhsh, Paul H Rubin and Joanna M Shepherd, Emory University Paper, 2003. P18: 1 George W Bush, State of the Union Address, 20 Jan 2004; 2 Martin Narey quoted in *The Observer* (London), 5 May 2002; 3 UN High Commission for Human Rights, Standard Minimum Rules for the Treatment of Prisoners, first adopted in 1955. P9: 1 Peter Olohan, USA quoted in 'Is prison the best punishment? Your reaction' BBC online Talking Point, 10 Sep 1998: http://newswww.bbc.net.uk/1/hi/talking_point/168607.stm (4/7/05) 2 Matt Salmon, quoted in Klass Action Review, Autumn 1998, Vol. 4, No. 3; 3 Wendy Utting. P20: YES 1 US Constitution: Sixth Amendment; 2 Baroness Helena Kennedy, QC, 'Law Reforms Show "Disdain For Public" by Lee Gordon, Camden New Journal, 21 Nov 2002; 3 Robert D Myers, Ronald S Reinstein and Gordon M Griller, Complex Scientific Evidence and the Jury, Judicature, Vol 83(3), Nov-Dec 1999; NO 1 Lord Falconer, 'Trial by Jury is it under threat': http://www.pcs.org.uk/Templates/Internal.asp?NodeID=884710 (4/7/05); 2 From court transcripts, Sacremento, California, 25 November 1997; 3 Professor Richard Dawkins, 'Three herring gull chicks ... the reason juries don't work' *The Observer* (London), 16 Nov 1997. P22: 1 Karen MacNutt, 'Posted', Women & Guns': http://www.womenshooters.com/archive/old1103issue/macnutt1103.html (4/7/05); 2 Second Amendment, US Constitution; 3 Gary A Mauser, 'The Failed Experiment, Gun Control and Public Safety in Canada, Australia, England and Wales' *Public Policy Sources*, A Fraser Institute Occasional Paper, Number 71 / Nov 2003. P23: 1 National Rifle Association of America from FBI data: http://www.nraila.org/Issues/FactSheets/Read.aspx?ID=18 (4/7/05); 2 Transcript of John Howard interview With Philip Clark, Radio 2GB on 17 Apr 2002: http://www.pm.gov.au/news/interviews/2002/interview1600.htm (4/7/05); 3 Anne Pearson, 1996 4 Million Mom March: http://www.millionmommarch.org/about (01/07/05). P24: 1 James Douglas-Hamilton, Speech to Conference 2002: http://www.scottishtories.org.uk/conference/conf02-lordjd-h.html (01/07/05); 2 Grant Mcnally, Parliament of Canada: http://www.parl.gc.ca/37/2/parlbus/chambus/house/debates/049_2003-01-30/han049_1835-E.htm (01/07/05); 3 Jeanette Basl, quoted on: http://www.crimevictimsunited.org/measure11/measure11arguments.htm (01/07/05). P25: Judge David A. Young, Circuit Court for Baltimore City, 5 Jun 1998, quoted in 'Trying Children In Adult Courts' Human Rights Watch: http://www.hrw.org/reports/1999/maryland/Maryland-02.htm; 2 Barry Feld, quoted in 'Adult crime, juvenile time' *Philadelphia Inquirer*, 14 Mar 2004; 3 Lisbet Palme, 'No age of innocence: Justice for children', UNICEF: http://www.unicef.org/pon97/protec1c.htm (04/07/05). P26: NO 1 Lisa Stevens, 9 Jan 2003; 2 Ann Widdecombe, 'Widdecombe: Together we can win war against crime', speech on 22 May 2001: http://www.conservatives.com/tile.do?def=news.story.page&obj_id=10538&speeches=1&type=print; (04/07/05); 3 Ron Lovelock, 'Borstal changed my life', 17 Oct 2002: http://news.bbc.co.uk/2/low/uk_news/2330061.stm (04/07/05); YES 1 Lord Bingham, giving evidence to the select committee on Home Affairs, 17 Mar 1998; 2 The National Mental Health Association, 'Juvenile Boot Camps': http://www.nmha.org/children/justjuv/bootcamp.cfm (04/07/05); 3 Lucie Russell, Press release from SmartJustice, 29 July 2003. P28: 1 Tasmania Police: www.police.tas.gov.au/police/police2001.nsf/W/Resources/CCAS-5GG8KL/?Open; 2 Essex police quoted in 'Decoy cars will be first in the country', Kim Perks, 16 May 2002: http://213.210.6.88/crimedatabase/site/content.php?article_id=339 (05/07/05); 3 Kevin Mills quoted in 'Car Thefts Crackdown': http://www.southyorks.police.uk/ serving_you/ServingYouPg03SheffNorth.pdf (05/07/05); 4 Bob Hastings quoted in 'Police urge better parenting after crash of joy-riding teens' by Jamie Berry, *The Age* (Australia), 15 Aug 2003. P29: William McCRea; 2 BBC online talking point, Sep 2002, 3 Insurance Bureau of Canada: http://www.ibc.ca/ii_auto_theft_8.asp. P30: 1 Craig A. Anderson, 'Violent Video Games: Myths, Facts, and Unanswered Questions', *Psychological Science Agenda*, Volume 16: No. 5, Oct 2003; 2 Mary Lou Dickerson, Washington State Department of Health Press Release, 2000; 3 Barbara Biggins, ABC TV, 16 Sep 2003. P31: 1 Neil Seeman, 'In Defense of Video Games', CANSTATS, 8 March 2004: http://www.canstats.org/readmore.asp?sNav=pb&id=640 (05/07/05); 2 Douglas Lowenstein quoted in 'Video games back in US dock' by Rachel Clarke, BBC News online, 15 Sep 2003: http://news.bbc.co.uk/1/hi/technology/3104892.stm (05/07/05); 3 Computer Games and Australians Today Project, Office of Film and Literature Classification, December 1997. P32: 1 'Crime Stats Show That Government Must Tackle Binge Drinking', 21 July 2004: http://www.polfed.org/FinalCS.pdf; 2 Millie Webb, spokeswoman for MADD: www.madd.org; 3 Theodore Dalrymple, City Journal, 2 May 2003. P33: Mr Justice Wood, quoted in 'Sentencing Aboriginal Offenders', 1992: www.legalaid.nsw.gov.au/data/portal/ 00000005/public/16163001099456570562.doc (05/07/05); 2 Quoted in: http://csswashtenaw.org/ada/resources/community/poster_words.html (05/07/05); 3 Dr Garry Slapper, *Times Newspapers*, 2003: http://www.ias.org.uk/publications/alert/97issue1/alert9701_p6b.html (05/07/05). P34: YES 1 Western Australian Aboriginal Justice Agreement, Mar 2004; 2 Pennsylvania Supreme Court Committee Report on Racial and Gender Bias in the Justice System, 2002; 3 Amnesty International: http://www.amnesty.ca/usa/racism.php (05/07/05); NO 1 Justice Frank Williams quoted in 'No Racial Discrimination in RI Courts, Chief Justice Says': http://www.insidepolitics.org/heard/heard081201.html (05/07/05); 2 BBC online talking point, Jun 2002. P36: 1 Sir Keith Morris quoted in *The Guardian* (London), 4 July 2001; 2 Fulton Gillespie, speaking to Home Affairs Select Committee on Drugs, May 2002, 3 Transform Drug Policy Foundation, June 2004 briefing. P37: Drug Watch International: http://www.drugwatch.org/T&L%20Drug%20Legalization.htm (05/07/05); 2 'Responses Of President George W. Bush', Joint Centre for Political and Economic Studies, 2004: http://www.jointcenter.org/2004election/Presidential-Survey-Bush-Response.pdf (05/07/05); 3 *The Observer* (London), Feb 2005; 4 Thaksin Shinawatra, 24 Mar 2003 quoted on: http://t2web.amnesty.r3h.net:80/pages/tha-010304-action-eng (05/07/05). P38: 1 Sean Silverthorne, 'Music Downloads: Pirates – or Customers?' 21 Jun 2004: http://hbswk.hbs.edu/item.jhtml?id=4206&t=innovation (05/07/05); 2 May 2002, © David Strom, Inc: http://www.strom.com/awards/287.html (05/07/05); Russell Simmons, Cyberposium 2003 conference, 18 Jan 2003. P39: 1 Britney Spears, quoted in 'Britney, Nelly, Missy Elliott Want You To Quit Stealing Music', 26 Sep 2002: http://www.mtv.com/news/articles/1457802/20020926/spears_britney.jhtml (05/07/05); 2 Matraca Berg, Music United 2003; 3 David Munns quoted in 'EMI boss defends music industry; Universal drops prices', The Daily Roxette, 4 September 2003: http://www.dailyroxette.com/article.php/1375; 5 Recording Industry Association of America: http://www.riaa.com/news/newsletter/082602.asp (05/07/05); 6 Professor Felix Oberholzer-Gee and Koleman Strumpf, 'The Effect of File Sharing on Record Sales', Mar 2004. P40: YES 1 Susan Herman, Press release about parallel justice project, 30 Oct 003; 2 Tony Blair, Press Conference, 25 Oct 2004; 3 Government of South Australia, 2001 © Attorney-General's Dept; NO 1 John Wadham, BBC News, September 2003 2 Israeli Supreme Court, 1996; 3 Article 11, UN Declaration of Human Rights. P42 NO: 1 Lesley Martin quoted in 'To help someone die gently', 31 Mar 2004: http://www.news24.com/News24/World/News/0,,2-10-1462_1506038,00.html; 2 Ludwig Minelli on BBC 'Newsnight', 2002; 3 Ronald Dworkin, Life's Dominion – An Argument About Abortion and Euthanasia, Harper Collins, 1993; YES 1 Pro-Life Alliance, *The Observer* (London), 5 December 2004; 2 International Task Force on Euthanasia and Assisted Suicide © 1996–2004; 3 Tara Flood, speaking to the parliamentary select committee, 2004

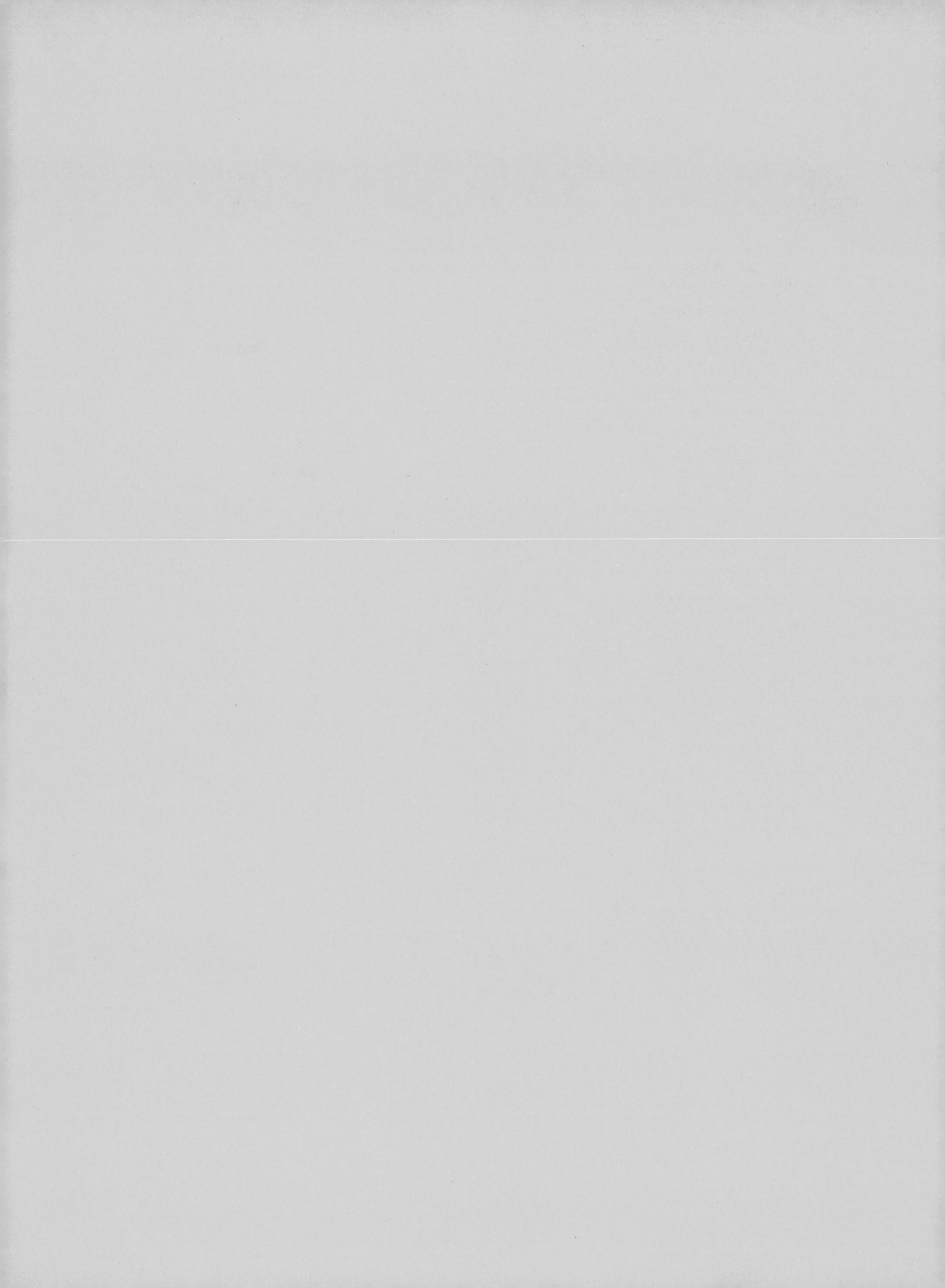